W9-BGN-056

FIRST & LAST

FIRST & LAST

Poems

by

Rennie McQuilkin

Antrim House

Simsbury, Connecticut

Library of Congress Control Number: 2005909369

ISBN: 0-9770633-2-1

Printed in the United States of America

by Van Volumes, Ltd

First edition, 2006

Front cover photograph by Eleanor McQuilkin Burns

Back cover photograph by Pit Menousek Pinegar

Antrim House

www.antrimhousebooks.com

860.217.0023

ACKNOWLEDGEMENTS

Fellowships from the National Endowment for the Arts and the Connecticut Commission on the Arts have been invaluable. Thanks to those sponsors of the arts and to all who have offered advice over the years, in particular members of the writing groups to which I have belonged: Charles Darling, Steve Foley, Emily Holcombe, David Holdt, Elizabeth Kincaid-Ehlers, Susan Lukas, Pam Nomura, Hugh Ogden, Pit Pinegar, and Drew Sanborn. Special thanks to my wife, Sarah, and to Norah Pollard, who both made very useful suggestions. Thanks also to editors of the following magazines and journals that first published poems contained in this volume, usually in earlier versions:

The Atlantic Monthly: "Twelve"
Beloit Poetry Journal: "Cecropia," "Home Burial" (as "Burial")
Chelsea: "Henri Raymond Marie de Toulouse-Lautrec-Montfa," "Home Birth"
College English: "The Pass," "The Zenith"
Common Ground Review: "First & Last"
Connecticut Poetry Review: "The Release"
Connecticut Review: "For Rosa Robata"
The Literary Review: "Lines"
Margie, The American Journal of Poetry: "On Assignment in Uganda"
Ontario Review: "The Naming"
Pembroke Magazine: "And God Bless Harry Walker"
Poet Lore: "The Dealer"
Poetry: "At the Bar," "Bruegel's Players," "Doing Time at Gilead Regional," "Eviction," "His Hands" (as "Hands"), "An Old Man's Sense"
Poetry Daily (on-line)*:* "An Old Man's Sense," "Bruegel's Players"
Poetry Northwest: "Baptism," "The Steam, the Steam"
The Recorder: "St. Gregory of the Golden Mouth"
The Southern Poetry Review: "First Snow in the Garden of the Geishas"
The Spoon River Poetry Review: "First Day"
Wind Literary Journal: "In Conclusion"
The Yale Review: "The Undoing"

Certain poems in this collection, sometimes in earlier versions, appear in *We All Fall Down* (Swallow's Tale Press), *Passage* (Antrim House), and *Private Collection* (Antrim House).

These poems are for Sarah

who has been so much a part of them.

TABLE OF CONTENTS

FIRST DAYS

PARENTAL

REVERSIONS

TABLE OF CONTENTS

We shall not cease from exploration
And the end of all our exploring
Will be to arrive where we started
And know the place for the first time.
Through the unknown, remembered gate
When the last of earth left to discover
Is that which was the beginning;
At the source of the longest river
The voice of the hidden waterfall
And the children in the apple-tree...

—T.S. Eliot, FOUR QUARTETS

FIRST DAYS

HOME BIRTH

for Benjamin

The cord was around your neck
when you were born
blue. A spring blizzard raged.

You survived, and the weather
turned, but four-foot drifts
are up to the bird feeder

where the cat digs in, hunkers,
and deep in her throat makes
bird noise: ruffles, clever trills.

The birds know, except a junco
comes close,
too close, is left for me

to finish off. I turn to you,
my shadow falling on the crib.
You sound too like the bird.

I look elsewhere,
concentrate on the egg shine
of dawn I woke to this morning,

magnified wings silhouetted,
otherworldly
on the window shade: starlings

in love with construction,

scratching snow from the gutter,
working a wattle of twigs, singing,

mocking whatever deconstructs—
a rattle of snow plow,
snarl of chain saw, birdcall of cat.

May a starling be your totem, Ben.
May false ruffles and trills have
nothing to do with you.

FIRST DAY

His tongue is too thick
to round out a word he tries
for days—*sko, skoo, skooo.*

When it's time
to give him to his teacher,
he happily waves me off.

I find him later
by the swings, spilled.
The others stare, sharp-eyed

at him, head pulled in,
hands up
by his ears, legs tucked.

In the car I kiss
his too broad forehead.
Last summer

I showed him how
a morning glory, tight shut,
dark as a bruise, if warmed

by hand and breathed upon,
springs open, blue verging
on indigo.

He had me do it over

and over. Always the miracle.
We laughed and laughed.

Hands cupping his tight face,
I remember
hard enough for both of us.

CARRIE WOLF

She was a disgrace—kept hogs in her cellar
and chickens everywhere.

Nights, she rocked on her porch with a .22
the better to get a bead on the varmints
gnawing her pea patch, and children too.

Out of season things grew.
It wasn't right. Come May, her chestnut
looked like Christmas, and we knew

why. Any day they'd hang her from it,
a witch who had it coming when we heaved
the worst we had at her on Halloween.

And what she did
when she caught us filching the biggest
luckiest nuts her chestnut grew,

what she did
was she gave us sacks and a helping hand
and—

Carrie, that was fine burlap
you saved for us. You shouldn't have.

AND GOD BLESS HARRY WALKER

After I godblessed everyone
and mother left
I godblessed Harry Walker

because when the siren wailed
and Miss Berger rushed us down
below, past the furnace room
and Harry's closetful of mops

and lined us up
and made us sit small
with our heads bowed
and hands around our knees,

I knew the Luftwaffe wouldn't
because Harry winked at me
and made circles around his ear.
And he would know

the way he did when Miss Berger
sent me to the principal
and Harry stiff-armed a salute
with a pushbroom under his nose
and a wicked grin for principals.

The last time I saw Harry Walker
they had him in a crib.
He couldn't move a thing.
But his eyes made circles
and I knew he had them licked.

TEN

Her brother builds the solar system
out of styrofoam, remote, not talking.
The planets are mostly done, brightly
attached to the sun, the rings of Saturn
in the works on a pasteboard brim.

Her answer is her mother's
abalone shell comb, pink jade earrings,
malachite pendant coiled to strike,
ruby, turquoise, sapphire rings
and cincture of green glass beads.

She jingles into the moonstone night,
stands unsure,
then slowly, then faster, begins to spin
around herself.

EVICTION

I kick the door open. Like a newsreel's
flash of numbers counting down,
followed by the latest from the war zone,
a sudden glare

becomes a sidewalk, traffic, the el.
Small reflection in Eccle the Baker's
window, I'm wearing my Sox cap over
a flyer's leather flaps,

also several coats, both of my holsters—
all I can take with me.
I aim one finger, thumb cocked,
at everyone staring at the odds

and ends of family—a broken loveseat,
a bureau leaking underwear,
a cracked table covered with maps
riffled by the wind—anywhere

I want to go. A boy is tugged past me
by his mother, she publicly
not looking, he backwards like an owl.
I fire and fire

and something, a mattress,
falls from a third story window,
kicks up a litter of trash—butt ends
and bits of glass.

One end dangles in the gutter.

The ticking is filthy
with stains, some fat and tailed, some
curled like grins.

I fire at these, at the window,
the sky.
And the sidewalk opens—
old Eccle drags a sack the size of me

to the hole,
pushes it in. Scuttle of clawfeet.
The wind rattles the maps—anywhere
I want to go.

ON ASSIGNMENT IN UGANDA

I focus my lens on the boy's upper lip
with its curve and cleft of love's bow
strung with a sweet line of lower lip.

He has turned from the broken wall of
a smoldering church, has taken in what
my camera has shot—hundreds

locked inside, charred piles of bone
sparkling with shards of stained glass.
He knew them.

He holds a sprig of rosemary
to breathe through, sweeten the stench.
It doesn't

keep his lower lip from trembling,
tightening, pulling away from the bow,
beginning to release a scream.

Let it be shrill
enough to shatter the lens I see through.

BAPTISM

Things keep going on the way they do
except one day in the middle of nothing
they don't.

I remember how hot it was—not a creak
from the windmill
and the Fords our folks had come in
steamed.

We stood around.
Our pockets were no place for hands,
they said, and wouldn't let us in the dark
of the barn or anywhere God wouldn't be
because the preacher was in the yard
to baptize whoever he could
in Tatums' water tank.

Six lined up.
I envied them the cool of their gowns
and the year or so they had on me
but not the way he dragged them under
and kept them there so long they bucked
like bullheads.

Mostly, I went along with the hymnbook
someone pushed at me
until he got to Ellen McGee,
held her under and didn't stop,
thinking maybe anything that pretty
was bound for goings on.

I was ready for something like the cat

I had tried to drown and failed
when up she came as sweet...
and stood for a spell at the edge
of the tank, at home in the sky.

And her gown, wet through, was true to her
and her face was where the sun had been.

TWELVE

A pretty good day, junk fish
and a couple of trout.
Friendly with muskrat
I drift, I cast at rings,

pass the '58 Chevy with fins,
stripped, a place to play
in which I once found
underthings.

What's up
around the bend
is flowers, and among them,
reaching for the sky,

legs,
some girl's, toes curling,
curling, nails red, her hair
a sight. The boy I forget.

CECROPIA

It wasn't butterflies I wanted, daytime flirts,
but moths, the shy ones furred and thick-fronded,
pale green, lavender, umber, rose-mottled giants
with the Maker's thumb print on their wings.
Polyphemus, Promethea, Luna, Io, Cecropia.

Luring such mystery with lantern light
the summer I was twelve, I saw across the street
the bride moon-white, bridesmaids pale green
dancing in the gold and navy night.

At sixteen I kept a harem of cocoons, their silk-
sacks swelling, also a '49 Kaiser convertible,
cow-horned, zebra-seated, two-tone red I polished
until I saw myself in it, crew-cut.

The day I was licensed I did 98
on NY 96, Ruth Ferguson drumming our song
on the dash. Gearing down for the turn onto Elm,
muffler shot, I backfired and backfired
for a girl rising up like that,
her arms in the air in a V and her fingers V's
and the plunge of her two-piece—oh lord!

Her parents were out.

When I pulled in, late, a Cecropia had hatched,
was half eaten by ants.
They blackened its bright new fur,
the sockets where eyes had looked for some way
out of this, the pink and umber wings,
too wet to fly.

SERVING GIRL WITH GALLANTS

after "A Woman Drinking with Two Men," Pieter de Hooch

First the checkered black and amber tile is applied
on the canvas, then leaded glass, stage right,
is made to admit enough of Delft's astonishing light
to gild the room. Soon it's time

for the tavern's newest treasure,
a slender young woman in maroon-red skirt,
tight-waisted purple tunic and linen-wimpled curls,
demure as the Virgin over the mantle. Half turned,

her small feet prim on a tile, precariously
she lifts her goblet and through its prism sees
those slapdash gallants at table, brushed in swiftly,
to whom she is to sing. The first taps his knee,

the other like a cricket rubs a pair of meerschaums,
winking. Judging by that red-plumed broadbrim
and orange, white-tasseled sash, they come from
the greater world of the provincial map behind them.

That the game is all, its players the usual
pawns, is lost on them, but we see from our remove
a pentimento of chessboard floor shine through
one dandy's handsome pair of oxblood boots.

Upstage, the old serving woman, eyes averted,
who brings a brazier of coals to warm the worldly
assumes her part is to be used. But the girl—
she holds up her goblet by its base uncertainly

as if to shed light on a dark passage. Her Rhenish,
kindling in a shaft of sunlight, trembles.

FIRST SNOW IN THE GARDEN
OF THE GEISHAS

Slowly, each flake discrete, a calligraph,
the snow descends on Kyoto.
The sky is a scroll,
its characters spelling the many names
of Buddha.

In this garden of the geishas, the snow
on japonica, laurel and stone
is elaborated
by the day's last sun, like the youngest geisha
adorned for song, for dance

and pleasures more expensive.
Her face, glazed white,
is deftly painted, kimono tied like a flower,
outlining her nape in red,
revealing the slightest hint of down.

In half an hour the paper lanterns will glow,
the plump-breasted plover on each
an invitation
to the narrow lane of Pontocho.
Half an hour and the shamisen will sound,

the feast begin. Now, she walks the garden,
its pattern blurred by the bright disguise
of snow. Beneath a pretty toy bridge
glide pinioned ducks like polished
courtesans in jade and coral and ivory.

As if to bow, she bends down
to roll a seed of snow
until it is fruit, white fruit.
It grows, unveils the grounds of the garden
where only a year ago she was a novice,

drank saki from the triple cup of love,
wore on her feet the bells
to which her hair, unbound at night,
fell softly as the lavender sleeves
of her kimono.

The dark descends,
the snow fruit glows, and above it
a full-faced moon, glazed white,
leaves the world behind. Far off,
a temple bell. Now the shamisen sounds.

FOR ROSA ROBATA

Auschwitz, 1944

Bone-thin, bald, sixteen, her job
packing gunpowder
in detonators, she steals an ounce

a day for the underground,
prays the sand she replaces it with
won't outweigh what she hides

in the one place they don't inspect.
Today she pushes the black seed in
too quickly.

The bride's sharp pain in her cry
gives her away. Then the stripping
and what the guard calls his

poetic justice, followed by the rope,
the scaffold's creak—her unborn
children begging to be unimagined.

BRUEGEL'S PLAYERS

after "The Hunters in the Snow," Pieter Bruegel the Elder

How bleak these three who trudge into town
with just one fox to show for the hunt,
their lean dogs slouching behind, heads down,
man and beast black against the sepia snow.

Above, a murder of crows waits patiently.
Only one of the houses sends up any smoke:
the people's firewood has been commandeered
for the Spanish garrison, there,

against those ice-blue cliffs. But look, oh see,
says Bruegel, the bliss
of a magpie sheering the verdigris
sky, and far below on the sky-green ice, children

skating—such tiny black ciphers enjoying
a touch of carmine for scarf, dot of pink for face.
Three of them chase a fourth; a small boy,
bent-kneed, makes a V

of his blades; another hunches down, spins a top.
Dark stroke, hands muffed, a young woman,
thin from starvation, stops
to watch. She commits the scene to memory.

THE ZENITH

There's always the tall dark
of the barn
to hide in, the mattressing
alfalfa, timothy, meadow grass.

Beyond the hickory stanchions
smooth as well-worked leather
from a century and more of cows,
beyond the Jerseys,
their mouths full of summer,
I climb a ladder to the mow
and from there to the cupola,
a rope.

Like any raccoon I settle down.
Everything comes in clearly—
a gabbling of frogs in the swamp,
a hoot owl in the pines,
June bugs banging the Coleman,

and now
maybe fifty stations on a Zenith,
an old one shaped like a church
I've put together tube by tube.

Grounded on a lightning rod
and wired to the cooling-room
that Zenith brings in the Tigers,
the Indians, the Pirates.
One by one I call them up,
in touch with everywhere.

PALEONTOLOGY

Scrupulous as a scholar slicing uncut pages of
a first edition, my grandson pares sheaves
of brittle slate.

He looks into the imprint of a Paleozoic fern
and, leaning closer,
a stalled bee, legs curled, resting for its next foray.

Nothing's ever lost, he tells me, not listening
to the growl and snarl of trail bikes
just over the crest of a hill.

They have come to a different
deposit—a wreckage of pickups and vans,
sodden brothels, doors gaping, hoods sprung,

discarded parts mixed with beer cans and shards
of glass in the weeds between the bikers' ruts.
Every windshield radiates

a glitter of cracks. And you, my boy, parsing
the old inscriptions—I fear
what the world that makes *this* will make of you.

DOING TIME AT GILEAD REGIONAL

I make my way through a wreck
of words, past Arabel and Tony
making out in the corner
of English 3H,
into the hall where Miss Bloom,
the principal, collars a girl—

Forget it. I hit the road.
Nice country here in E. Gilead
and spring to boot. Cows.
Sun on the run-off,
boulders like Dorsets,
Dorsets like boulders, geese
in the cornfield. Nice all right.

Except for these cabanas
where shackled calves do time,
the better to be tender veal,
reminding me

how after class Miss Bloom
collared that girl, late from Art
and running the hall, bearing
such gaudy eggs.

Out here in E. Gilead the cows
are lowing to no avail—the calves
are going nowhere. And I,
strapped in, no headroom
in my Civic, am just thinking

how the principal collared
that girl with the enameled
Easter eggs, lifted one
and looked into its window,
saw the tiny figures within
and smiled so

for a moment I fancied
the little people came and went
at will, their walls the world,
their case a precedent
for all of us—

until a buzzer sounded. Time
for History.

THE PASS

Plato put it well, like so—
beyond the particular is the permanent.
That is, beyond the arc of one dead jay I throw
to the woods (it hits a pine
and drops),

beyond such a broken arc
and the almost parabolic piss Davy Miller took
at recess and hit the drinking fountain
and got sent to Miss Ward—

beyond such arcs
is the one they all aim to be.
I think I saw it in November of '53.
It was the Blue against the Brighton 2's,
fourth quarter, tight,
when Number 3, George Nichols of the Blue

faded back in the mud, back
to the end of his own end zone
and got one off as he went down. It spirals still
to the 50 and into the arms of the wide end
who fakes and cuts and pulls it in, a peach.
He hardly has to look for the ball.

Behind him Nichols is down, his number's mud,
but what he threw
was just what Plato knew he would.

PARENTAL

HIS HANDS

for my father and his

One of his hands held the pulpit hard,
grew livid every Sunday.
The other aimed at the faithful.
Back and forth my father's hand would
rake us, mowing us down.

Like Abraham with Isaac overhead
he held the Host, then broke it.
The wafer, snapping, might have been
me, held up, an example.
Of course it wasn't. It was God.
Over and over God broke
beneath his hands.

When a cougar stopped our Franklin
ten miles beyond Carmel,
slow as the switch of the animal's tail
he reached for the tool box
on the running board,
and the cat didn't like the looks
of a hand that dogmatically raising
a hammer.

Moving east in '15, held up by snow
in the Sierras, my first,
we all got down from the Pullman.
I said it was Heaven
and I was an angel and could prove it.
Flat out in the snow, I beat my arms,

made wings
and sang the Alleluiah Chorus.

When I turned to take my punishment
there were iceballs in both his hands
and two in the air above.
He was juggling, juggling snow,
as sure of where we were as any angel.

THE UNDOING

I jump from crosstie to crosstie,
walk a humming rail. This
is forbidden.

Rounding a bend I'm interrupted
by a barn
through which the tracks run on—
a heavyset barn, hand hewn,
with a long row of panes
like unbroken eyebrows
above the open double doors.

Within, a boy is about to get what's
good for him. His hands are tied
to a post, shirt off, pants down.
They're mine.

I hear a belt slip through
its loops, its slap against a palm
like stropping a razor, the whisper
of the belt to the air, the hiss,
the crack. And what little I am
is less.

Then there's no buckle shining
like a badge, just the flash
of swallows, white of droppings.
The barn's roof is sagging,
slates broken.

I open a toolbox

I'm never to open, ever,
and see no tools,

just thick red sticks I set so well
that when I trigger the barn
the fall of debris is gentle, a good
growing rain.

THE NAMING

for C.L.F.

The summer I was twelve I began to know
the Bottom—old growth sycamores and willows
thick with furred and gnarling vines.
I dug root-raftered burrows in mud-hole banks,
bush-whacked my way

to a clearing and something more
or less than a house,
bark on its logs, guinea hens on its roof,
a sow with one eye open under it,
and rocking slightly, smiling crookedly

out front, not friendly, but amused
by the little savage come up from the Bottom,
a man who said *Huh*. That summer I learned
to grain the guineas, slop the hogs,
kick the sow in the snout for chewing my boot,

coil hooks with crayfish, pull in bullheads,
slice off their barbs
and gut them with a single scoop of the hand.
I wore a crow's feather in my hair,
sometimes a cat bird's, once an oriole's,

told no one
how Henry Minor taught me
to fox-bark, fire only once, cry the creature's
treble death cry, see the fox ghost hover
and ask of it a blessing.

Then school began and he got work

raising a suspension bridge between states,
walking sky beams, as he said.
Making more than's good for an Indian,
my father said.

I thought it was more the sky he wanted than
the money, but had to hear him say it
and didn't for the year he was gone,
then barely understood, the way he slurred
and turned away when he came back.

By now I was occupied with being thirteen
too much to mind. Who was he anyway?
Some drunken Indian. He deserved
the bottle-bomb I set off in his outhouse.
When he fired at me, I couldn't forgive him.

Or myself. Or whoever tore down his shack.
Or how he vanished and fifty years passed
before he surfaced in the obit it took
for me to start forgiving both of us. It's time
I called him by his proper name.

Cries Like A Fox,
come from where you hide at the wood's edge,
name me, tell me who I am, give me back
my feather of Crow,
feather of Cat Bird, feather of Oriole.

THE DANCE

for Robin

The wayback of the mind
is the brains
behind a dance like ours,
my son.

You come at me low down,
your hands turned horns.
I feint, unfurl a cape of air,
indent my back, unveil
the sword.

You gore me graciously,
I kill you con amore.

HOME BURIAL

A boy is in the field, digging,
whose father has been stunned by
the sledge of time, doesn't know

enough to drop or try again.
A boy is in the field, digging
a hole which is perfectly square,

whose father gets nothing straight,
not his crooked furrows,
his pretty wife, the truth.

A boy is in the field, digging
a hole which is perfectly square,
knowing all,

whose father didn't know
to keep old Moses from
bloating himself on half-ripe oats,

couldn't find the slugs
to shoot the horse
and had to use a maul.

A boy is in the field, digging
a hole which is perfectly square,
knowing all,

whose mother once swung him
flat out in the spinning world
and said she'd never let go, ever.

A boy is in the field, digging
a hole which is perfectly square,
knowing all

too well whose mother it was,
skirt up in the mow
with the hired man.

A boy is in the field, digging
a hole which is perfectly square,
knowing all

he can do is make it deep,
straight down enough
for more than a stiff-legged horse.

THE SILENCE

for Bix Beiderbecke, 1901-1927

Daisy Ellington held her son she called the Duke
to be a genius. He owed it to her
to become one.

Bismark Beiderbecke of Davenport didn't hold Bix
to be anything, stuffed his son's recordings,
unopened, in a closet.

In the end Bix went to his room in Queens
where he persevered night & day, directing fifths
of Jim Beam

at the cornice, swinging his bottle
from side to side in some Birdland of the mind—
his last cornet, so muted he died of the silence.

LATE START

for Norah Pollard

It was dark green
and leather-bound, with a brass lock,
fleurs-de-lis along the spine.

Nothing prepared you for your mother
when you showed it—"No money
for milk or bread, and you bought

that—Jesus, Mary and Joseph,
you're either the stupidest child alive
or the most selfish!"

Of course I don't know this yet
when I find you trudging by the river,
holding the journal at arm's length.

I praise what you're about
to hurl in the water, ask if you're
a writer,

and never minding you won't answer
show you the sycamore
leaning over Ten Mile River—

slats for rungs and a knotted rope
hung from a limb to which, grudgingly,
you climb. Despite yourself, you let

go, release a scream of fear or joy

or rage, and come up
kicking, arms flailing the current.

Then the laughter, mine and yours,
and your promise to write it all up
between the forbidden fleurs-de-lis...

All right, my part in that's a lie. Fact is
I was in another state. And many years
would pass before you made your entry

in a journal less promising than the one
you threw. But let's try it this way and
see what history makes of it.

LINES

for Dick Witte

It's only glass
I've broken. Mother goes on
licking a thread, pushing it at the eye,
face bunching like a club,
then heaves out of her chair and begins

to hit me
with a magazine, and when that shreds,
with her fists.

I can't forgive my father
for hiding
behind the paper, a big man twice
her size. As usual, he lets her happen,

doesn't say a thing.
She does the talking in that house.
My father is her cross, she says.
I can't forgive him
for not knowing better

and hide in the shed among the tools.
Today, he comes for me, has nothing
to say, just shows me
to the car. We reach the river,

and in the trunk beside his rod
I find a brand new Heddon Tru-flex
with a Shakespeare reel. From his coat

he pulls a Green Ghost,
Orange McKenzie, Royal Coachman.

How delicately, with a huge hand
battered and missing a finger, he threads
the silk through the shining eyes.

All afternoon we work the trout.
The only sounds
are those that slowly grow used to us
and the high song, long whisper
of lines.

First his, then mine, then sometimes
together, the lines arch out, and settle
exactly where we want them.

REVERSIONS

AN OLD MAN'S SENSE

of time is shot. Now he is five in Indian head dress
facing off with the boy across the street
and now he is being born. The frames

blur by—his small head crowning, coming to light
is an old man's, white on hospital
white. Now the film so quickly reeling and unreeling

jams. It fixes on a single frame.
Before a brilliant circle burns out from its center
he sees

a sleeping compartment
elegant in the velvet and brass-fitted style
of the overnight express from Algeciras to Madrid.

He is raising a tasseled, dark green window shade
on the full Spanish moon. The white of it spills
across the cream and umber landscape of his bride.

THE DEALER

Where neon announces
Flamingo Hilton, Hilton, Hilton
she deals exquisitely, says little.
What's it to her if you lose?
She's the house. Except sometimes

when a jackpot's splatter of coin
is goat's milk in an empty pail
and her fingers,
smart as whips with a double deck,
forget the deal, feel only the squeeze,
release and squeeze of a teat,

she's ten and no one's property.
It's dawn on the ridge
with the eggs to collect.
If she sneaks one, sucks the yolk,
no one will be the wiser, no one
will count the chips.

Whatever clouds loom
are what a child can make of them,
never puffed and whey-faced
supervisors staring down from
ceiling mirrors, corner mirrors
and catwalks everywhere.

THE STEAM, THE STEAM

Oh the steam there was back then—
a vapor in August from Egdahl's icehouse,
chunks of winter swaddled in sawdust,

and from the Empire State, just in,
Track 2, a steam that hissed
when I reached for the solid silver wheels.

There was sweet steam from the midst
of manure, sour smoke from piles of leaves
that smoldered damply all November,

and cold mornings
from fermenting mash I fed to boozing cows,
the steam, the steam.

What's left is a diesel's exhaust
where I idle today, waiting for the light at
4 & 10 in Farmington. I crank the window,

clear the fog,
breathe a ghost or two on the frozen air,
try different shapes. And a child

on her way to school in the car next door
won't be outdone. We enter into competition.
Oh the steam, the steam.

REVISION

A hard sleet rattles the sash
by which she naps,
strapped into a wheelchair.
What occupies her

is not weather, not where she is,
sixteen, painting and painting
St. Paul de Vence. This evening
the town's *chasseur du lapins*

throws pebbles at her window.
"Viens, viens!" From the cote
of the bell tower, the stroke
of the clapper startles a flock

of pigeons. They whirl
out and shine as she will
now, under a waxing moon.
Such sweet commotion

comes of silk on cotton
and buttons unbuttoned
she cannot hear the crisp
entry of an aid with dinner.

AT THE BAR

for N.S.

Two Jack Daniels, neat,
and you're less defunct, teeth
your own, kidneys a miracle.
It's time

to tell about the farm,
how your father glittered
as he stuck the dog-eared sow
you and a friend held down.
When her thrashing's a shudder,
two short kicks, a final thrust,

the story falters and you order
another round, try again.
Your father can scrub the hog
all he likes, can quarter
until she's merely ham to hang
in a smokehouse made
cleverly of crates—

your heart's no longer in it.
You stare at your hands, veins
standing out as black a blue
as the throat of the hog
hung up, head down, to drain.

HENRI RAYMOND MARIE DE
TOULOUSE-LAUTREC-MONTFA

It wasn't that simple.
Besides Henri and Toulouse and Lautrec
there were those other titles to live up to
and—if you asked Rosa la Rouge
or Madame Poupoule—
some spicy sobriquets as well: Big Spout,
Corkscrew.

So first, Henri,
communicant with certain birds and trees,
a child so beautiful his mother could cry—
the eyes especially, the eyes
in which his thoughts, like bright fish,
moved just below the surface.

Then Raymond—after his uncle the Count
who fell from a horse and died, humped over.
It ran in the family. For no better reason
he fell and broke himself, grew no taller
than a troll. Frog-lipped, enormously nosed,
he made a virtue of stunted limbs,
declared the world to be a circus
and he its dearest freak,
a man the whores would pay to serve.

He'd rise from a night with them
and one or two hours of sleep
to gather his tools, become Marie again
devoted to his copper plates and canvases.

But he never forgot he was a Toulouse

whose people had owned the south of France
and the ear of God. He was born to it,
would tell how his mother kept a bevy of nuns
in one of her chateaus, their only duty
to pray for his sins,
which he was therefore obliged to commit.

He was, after all, Lautrec ("low tricks,"
the envious English quipped). He loved
the drunks, the can-can girls, the aging whores,
was so much a part of the brothel where
he paid handsomely for bed, board and studio
he might have been a gilded ceiling mirror.
Mornings, he stole into their rooms
to sketch the bare-faced ladies before they woke.

At the height of his notoriety, suddenly
no one, Montfa of Montparnasse no more,
he closed up shop, and suffering from lesions,
painful swelling of the testicles and penis
as well as increasing spasms of hands and feet
and tumors in the brain inducing deafness,

went home.
Curled on the chaise longue at Malromé,
once more Henri, he asked for the songs
his mother had kept in mind for him,
the toy gazelle she'd saved, the silver crucifix.

ST. GREGORY OF THE GOLDEN MOUTH

*Born on Inis Mór in the Aran Islands, sent to Rome in
398. His coffin is said to have floated back to his birth-
place in Cill Rónáin. Not recognized by Rome.*

I was so pretty a pagan, the Abbot said, he'd have
me sent to Rome—it was a sin the way I cavorted
from crag to crag in uncured sandals
with the fur still bristling on their soles.

I let myself be sent, hating as I did
the stench of burning dung
that hovered like the Aran fog in small stone rooms
and the beat of the terrible rock-breaking waves

on which the brittle black currachs were tossed
like upended beetles, all six oars flailing.
My own father had been taken by the breakers
at Bungowla, dashed against the rocks and flayed,

brought home in pieces and puzzled together
by three crones keening like the wind
and warning me to kiss his frozen lips or be going
straight to hell.

His father's bones,
bits of gristle clinging, were dug from their patch
of dirt—old poverty of clay and crumbled stone—
for him to be planted in their place

and soon uprooted for the likes of me. I traded that
for the elegance of Rome, where my golden words
elevated me at the Vatican, the Celtic savage

civilized by velvet robes, at home

with the finest the City could offer,
drinking in the sweet marrow of its osso buco
washed down with papal wine. My new ways came
easily. Something lost must have risen in me

the way sweet-water on the Islands,
siphoned off by limestone swallow holes
to carve out underworlds,
will suddenly appear. This lasted thirty years.

I was not prepared, in the midst of Matins,
for the welling up
of Inis Mór's cursive, lacework walls
the early sun shone through, embellishing,

wives waiting on the beach at Cill Mhuirbhigh,
circled in mauve or red by their rings of skirt,
and a stone-gray pony backlit on a crag
above Dún Eochla, mane cresting like the surf.

This morning as I served communion, I saw
a coffin lengthen to a currach
bearing my gray and glittering remains
to three islands brightly green on a wine-dark sea.

FIRST & LAST

From a cranked crib she squints
at her great grandson—
blips of ultrasound on the Sony.

Skin taut, translucent,
mouth a dry well, she seems now
to see him—there,

the quick heart's dark bubbling,
bright little links of spine
supple

as fish,
a black and white skull to which
she nods hello.

NATIVITY SCENE

Christmas Eve, 2003

Arms locked around my neck, mother
foxtrots painfully from commode to bed,
a dozen tiny stutter-steps to each of mine,

a plastic tube to breathe through
trailing behind umbilically. I sponge-bathe
every part of her, never as close

since my other nursing. Later,
attending in the dim light of an Advent
candle, immersed

in the two-beat time of oxygen,
its pulse my own in the blood-warm dark,
I float in a world where birth is all.

IN CONCLUSION

for Lib, 1907-2000

Their heads and shoulders hover
like clouds, some bright,
some dark. I hear the mourning
in their bedside manners,

cannot tell them
I am dumb with delight,
going on ten, going for the mail,
curling my double-jointed big toe

around small stones,
wishing on each and letting fly
at trees and telephone poles,
then dipping the big tin pail

in the well, tipping it to me
and drinking
until my teethe ache, seeing
my braids surrounded by sky.

The water tastes of cedar, of moss.
Now the clouds move in,
the small insistent buzz of summer
diminishes.

THE RELEASE

for Naomi, 1932-1999

All around me, loved ones
are turning pale
as if their life support
has been removed.

Far off, I hear them say
their blessings and goodbye,
goodbye.
There is nothing I can do

for them. I'm six, and down
with measles.
It's dark, curtains
drawn. Now a single ray

shines from the door
where father's hands enter,
cupping what
they slowly release—wings

so pale a green they're all
but white, floating down
the ray to my open hand,
palm up. How light

the wings. They open, shut
and open, releasing me.

Rennie McQuilkin's poetry has appeared in publications such as *The Atlantic, The Southern Review, The Yale Review, The Hudson Review, Poetry,* and *The American Scholar.* He is the author of nine poetry collections, two of which have won awards, and his *New and Selected Poems* will be issued in 2007. He has received fellowships from the National Endowment for the Arts as well as the Connecticut Commission on the Arts, and for many years he directed the Sunken Garden Poetry Festival, which he co-founded at Hill-Stead Museum in Farmington, CT. In 2003 he received a Lifetime Achievement Award from the Connecticut Center for the Book.

To order additional copies
of *First & Last*
or other Antrim House titles
contact the publisher at

Antrim House
P.O. Box 111
Tariffville, CT 06081
860-217-0023
www.antrimhousebooks.com
eds@antrimhousebooks.com